DuPONT JUNIOR HIGH
RESOURCE CENTER
BELLE, W. VA.

Mark Trail's CAMPING Tips

Created by
Ed Dodd

Mark Trail's CAMPING Tips

Created by
Ed Dodd

AN ESSANDESS SPECIAL EDITION
New York

MARK TRAIL'S CAMPING TIPS
SBN 671-10354-7
Copyright, ©, 1969
by Publishers-Hall Syndicate.
All rights reserved.

Published by
Essandess Special Editions,
a division of
Simon & Schuster, Inc.,
630 Fifth Avenue, New York, N.Y. 10020,
and on the same day in Canada
by Simon & Schuster of Canada, Ltd.,
Richmond Hill, Ontario.
Printed in the U.S.A.

MARK TRAIL'S CAMPING TIPS 5

If you're planning to buy camping equipment, it's a good idea to rent your outfit first or go on a trip with someone who has equipment.

In this way you will find out what you need and avoid the purchase of unnecessary or inadequate articles.

Before loading hundreds of pounds of camping equipment on top of or in your auto, check with a garage or service station operator to see if you need any sort of rear suspension to help support extra weight.

Improving the rear suspension aids in handling, braking, and general resistance to the wear and tear of a loaded car.

CAMPING TIPS

When in public camp grounds, try to avoid driving nails into trees to hang equipment or erect any structures. These nails are not easily removed, and when they are pulled out, the holes leave the trunk exposed to further damage from water and insects.

If you plan to sleep in your station wagon when camping, carry along some mosquito netting to provide screens for windows. Drape material over open door, then close it to secure top of netting. The bottom edge and sides can be held down with tape.

CAMPING TIPS 9

After locating a campsite, survey it carefully and plan your layout before unloading your auto. Remember, too, that your car can be positioned to give you some protection and privacy.

An experienced camping friend of mine recommends putting up your cook fly before going to work on your tent. This will allow you to unload your auto and place equipment and supplies under a shelter in case of rain. Reverse the procedure when breaking camp.

CAMPING TIPS 11

I find that a miner's tent
is easier to pitch if it has a
sod cloth sewn around the bottom edge
rather than one with a floor sewn in.
This permits camping on uneven ground,
and the sod cloth may be tucked
under a separate ground cloth
for insect protection.

To prevent tripping over stakes near doorway of tent, use L-shaped steel stakes driven in flush with the ground.

CAMPING TIPS 13

To prevent metal tent stakes from rusting during storage, clean and dry them thoroughly. Then wrap them in an oily rag and store in a fireproof place.

Heavy fishing sinkers fastened to the corners of tent flaps help to keep them open or closed without continual flapping. Safety pins or a fishing line can be used to fasten sinkers to flaps.

CAMPING TIPS 15

Dark-colored tents absorb the sun's rays and are sometimes unbearable in hot climates. One way of cooling that works quite well is to cover the tent top with a white sheet to reflect the heat away from the tent.

If your tent has no floor,
a good way to keep dampness out of
your gear is to lay it on a piece of canvas
and fold ends as shown. Clothespins
snapped over the folded corners
will keep them together.

CAMPING TIPS 17

To avoid punctures and rot,
don't roll stakes or tent frame
with your tent; keep them separate.
Heavy rubber bands from an old inner
tube are excellent for
holding stakes, frames, and other
loose items together.

To prevent rain from
seeping into your tent from the
pole hole, cover it with aluminum foil,
waxed paper, or even a disk
from an old inner tube.
A rubber band can be used
to help secure covering.

CAMPING TIPS 19

Tents that leak around the seams can be temporarily repaired by applying rubber cement over the faulty areas. Apply several coats, allowing each coat to dry thoroughly.

Another use for that versatile poncho is as a "porch" fly in front of your wall tent. Lash an extra length of sapling to ridgepole, and secure ends of poncho with guy ropes, as shown.

CAMPING TIPS

To keep dirt or snow from getting into your tent, make a "doormat" of pine or cedar boughs.
In Southern regions, palmetto leaves make good doormats.

To keep your cooking area shielded from cold wind and rain, staple heavy plastic sheeting around canvas fly. Fold top edge of plastic as shown, before stapling. When breaking camp, simply pull sheeting free from staples. On the next trip, staple in another place along edge.

CAMPING TIPS 23

Shower curtain hooks are very useful around camp. I use them inside my tent for stowing my lantern out of the way, for hanging towels, clothing, equipment, etc.

When repairing your tent, a spoon will help you to push the needle through heavy canvas. Bend spoon around your hand and push on needle, as shown.

CAMPING TIPS 25

Knots often tighten and become difficult to untie in wet weather. To remedy this, place a small stick through knot when tying. When stick is removed, the resulting slack will make knot easy to untie.

To keep tents from tightening up during damp weather, cut an old auto inner tube into 3-inch strips; fasten strips together in pairs using clothesline rope, then fasten to tent guy lines, as shown.

CAMPING TIPS

When picking your campsite, it is best to avoid ravines, lowlands, or dry stream beds. Cloudbursts occurring miles away may cause dangerous flash floods without warning. Also, lowlands are more likely to be damp and infested with annoying insects.

When pitching camp, be sure to locate fireplace downwind from tent so that smoke and sparks will be carried away from it.

Place fire at least 10 feet away from your shelter, and clear away inflammable material from the area.

CAMPING TIPS

In an emergency, the parabolic reflector of your flashlight can be used to start a fire.

SHREDDED BARK OF RED OR WHITE CEDAR, UNRAVELED HEMP ROPE, ETC.

Place tinder through the bulb hole and point reflector toward the sun so that the rays will converge in center, igniting fire starter.

A roll of tissue soaked in mineral
spirits, kerosene, or bacon fat, then
placed in a coffee can or similar container
and ignited, makes a long-lasting
fire torch for extra light in camp, or
for use as an insect repellent.

Drain tissue before lighting,
and be sure torch is set a safe distance
from fuel container.

CAMPING TIPS

For protection from flies around your camp cooking area, a screen-covered food box or a piece of cheesecloth may be used.

You can build a flytrap of screen wire, using the simple inverted-cone principle. With a piece of tainted meat as bait, it will attract most of the flies in the area.

CAMPING TIPS 33

Before blowing up your air mattress, place a small piece of muslin (cut from a bandage in your first-aid kit) over the valve.

The cloth will prevent moisture from getting into mattress and possibly causing damage later.

One way to locate a small hole in your air mattress is to blow it partially full of smoke; then squeeze the mattress, and smoke will escape through hole.

CAMPING TIPS

In damp weather, prop your bedding off the tent floor with sticks when not in use so that it will remain dry and be more comfortable at night.

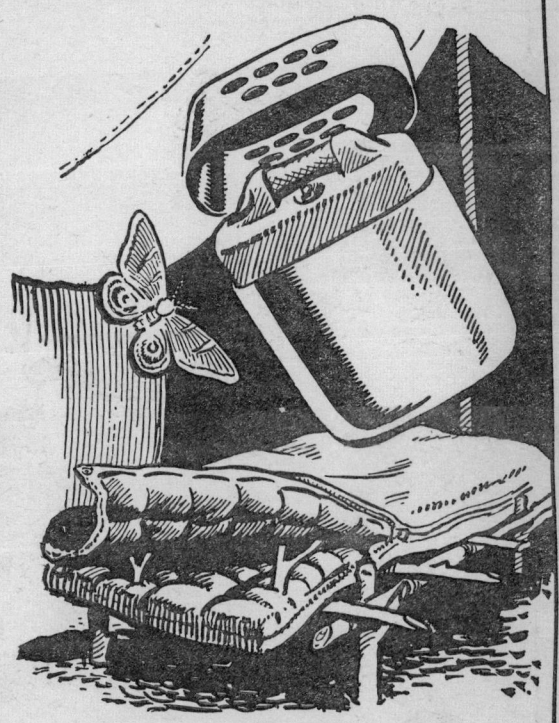

A couple of hand warmers that burn lighter fluid will help to dry out a sleeping bag should it become damp; prop open bag and place warmers inside.

Folding camp cots tend to be cold
because of the air space under them.
During cold weather, use ground sheets
of plastic or rubber, and sleep with
as many thicknesses of blankets under
you as you have on top of you.
Keep in mind, too, that a canvas
cot will sag badly if used
continuously as a chair.

CAMPING TIPS 37

As a safety precaution, a gasoline lantern or stove should be filled and lighted outside a tent or other small shelter.

Place such equipment where it will not be knocked over.

If you have a stove in your tent or shelter, be sure you have plenty of ventilation; monoxide poisoning has caused fatal camping accidents.

Should your tent be covered during a heavy blizzard, clear away snow so air can circulate through fabric.

CAMPING TIPS

Two 5-gallon cans may be made into a small tent stove. Cut tops off and slide one into the other. Use small bolts and nuts to join parts. Fit stovepipe into hole on top side of can.

CUT A DOOR IN BASE, FIT HINGE AND LATCHES...

HOLE FOR DRAFT

Be sure you have adequate ventilation when you are using your camp stove in an enclosed shelter.

Annoying fumes from an oil-burning heater may be neutralized by putting an orange peel on top of heater.

CAMPING TIPS

Hot coals from your campfire placed in a large tin can will keep your tent warmer in freezing weather. Set container on stones to prevent the tent floor from burning.

Before setting out on a camping trip, experiment in the kitchen with food servings so that you pack only what is needed.

For instance, a pound of coffee will brew 40 to 50 cups; half a cup of rice will make 3 servings; one cup of rolled oats makes 3 to 6 servings, and bacon will average about 20 slices to a pound.

CAMPING TIPS 43

Instead of throwing away your old cooking grill, separate the steel cross sections so you can use them on your camping trip as a cooking grate. Make a canvas case to carry them in your pack.

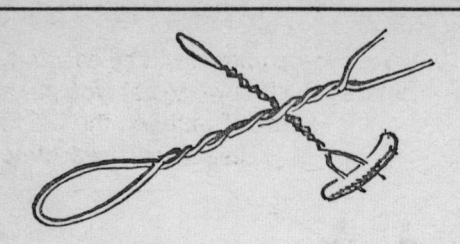

Here are a few outdoor cooking utensils which you can make from wire coat hangers.

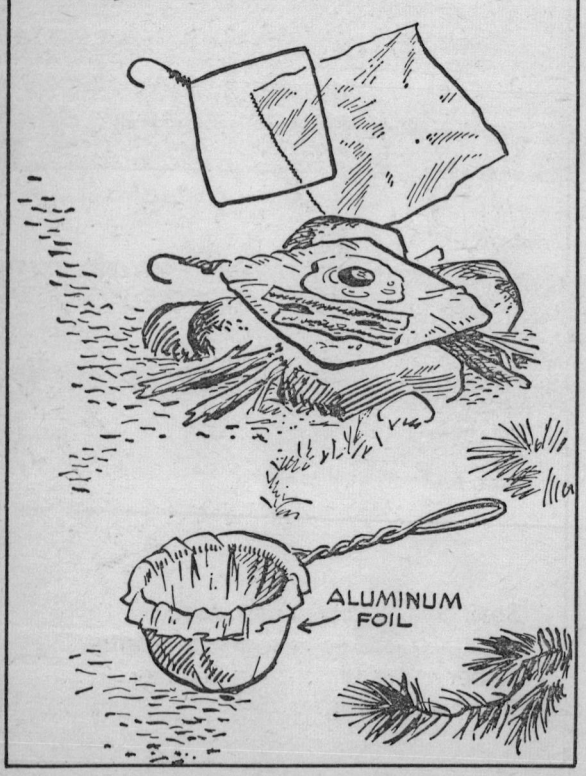

ALUMINUM FOIL

CAMPING TIPS

Your camp chores will be easier if, before you sit down to eat, you put a kettle of water on the fire to heat for dishwashing.

Soak utensils containing stuck or burned food scraps. Before retiring, gather and store kindling wood for the next morning.

White wood ash from hickory, beech, etc., makes a good substitute for soap when cleaning greasy pots, pans, and dishes. The ashes contain potash and soda and, when combined with a little hot water and elbow grease, can clean almost anything.

CAMPING TIPS

To avoid inconvenience during cooking or after dark, the efficient camper fills stoves and lanterns with fuel every day. Also, at suppertime, fill vacuum bottles with your favorite beverage and you will have a hot drink at night without the trouble of preparation.

To reduce the black smoke from lampwicks, soak them in vinegar and let them dry thoroughly before using.

CAMPING TIPS 49

If you can find the space, take along several portable folding stand trays on your next camping trip. They have many uses, including serving as a washstand for dirty dishes or hands.

Old mail-order catalogs or city phone books are worth their weight on a camping trip. The pages are fine for starting fires, cleaning greasy spots from pots and pans, and as place mats, emergency paper towels, etc.

CAMPING TIPS 51

For a handy, efficient camp toaster, cut top and bottom from a can just large enough to balance two edges of a bread slice. This toaster may be placed directly on burner or coals.

Your icebox will be more
efficient if you precool it before
leaving home by loading it with ice cubes
from the refrigerator. Some
campers put the icebox in their home
freezer for a day or so before
leaving on a camping trip.

CAMPING TIPS

If you do not have a reflector oven for baking bread, etc., in camp, you can make one from a large cylinder-shaped tin can. Make a cut, as shown, and fold back cut section to form a shelf for placing foods.

Any of the following methods can be used to purify water that is suspect:
1. Boil the water briskly for 15-20 minutes. Add 2 or 3 drops of tincture of iodine to each quart of water.
2. Certain laundry bleaches are suitable for purifying water in an emergency. Proportions to use are usually stated on the label.
3. Halazone tablets (purchased at drug store), and used according to directions on bottle.

CAMPING TIPS 55

A convenient way to prepare coffee and lighten your load is to mix ingredients at home:
- 1 part instant coffee
- 1 part dry "cream"
- 1 part sugar

Test proportions to suit your taste; then, in camp, simply put 3 teaspoonful of mixture in a cup and fill with hot water.

Since appetites increase alarmingly in the wilds, plan on larger food rations than you would eat at home. Take more sugar and more fats than you would normally eat, especially for higher altitudes.

CAMPING TIPS 57

If you plan to camp in extremely cold weather, it is wise to carry food that will not freeze too hard to eat or cook.

Before leaving home, food can be chopped to bite size. Dehydrated eggs and dried foods are good. Also, freeze-dried foods are no problem since they have no moisture in them to freeze.

To keep a loose
thermos cork from working itself out,
wet it, then sprinkle sugar on it
before inserting.

CAMPING TIPS

Fresh eggs can be kept in camp for several days without refrigeration by carrying them in your thermos bottle. Break eggs into bottle before leaving; then you can pour the eggs out as needed in camp.

Bacon will keep without refrigeration for a longer period of time on a camping trip if it is kept as a large slab instead of individual slices. Keep slab wrapped in a vinegar-soaked cloth until ready to use.

CAMPING TIPS 61

Wrapped in aluminum foil, your game bird or chicken can be roasted whole without losing tasty juices. Turn every 15 minutes and when done, remove foil and allow bird to brown over hot coals.

Here are a few forest fire safety rules
you should be aware of at all times
in the woods:
1. Never throw lighted smoking material out of a car window.
2. Sit down to smoke in the woods.
3. Use a lighter instead of matches.
4. Put your fire completely out — and drown it.

CAMPING TIPS 63

If there are no means of disposing of garbage in your camping area, burn all the scraps that you can in your campfire, then bury remains. Crush cans flat, as animals sometimes dig up litter and may get their heads caught in open containers.

Grease stains on clothing or camping gear can be removed more easily when petroleum jelly is applied.

Instead of allowing the grease to sink in, you can use petroleum jelly to soften the stain for more effective laundering.

CAMPING TIPS 65

Heavy woolen shirts often cause chafing and itching around the collar. Next time try dusting a little cornstarch around your neck.

After washing your woolen outdoor shirts, hang them to dry without wringing out the rinse water and they won't shrink.

To keep the toes of your boots from curling, try placing a pop bottle inside the foot. People with big feet may have to use the "giant-size" bottles.

CAMPING TIPS

Keep an extra pair of socks handy for comfortable sleeping in camp. Always put on the fresh pair before going to bed. The socks you have worn with boots will be damp with perspiration and will make your feet even colder than no socks at all.

A zippered plastic pillowcase makes a good camp suitcase, for the contents may be easily found. It is also good for soiled camp clothes.

CAMPING TIPS

If you wear several pairs of socks under your boots, be sure each pair is successively larger in length and width. However, socks that are too large make folds that may cause injury.

If your feet hurt in extremely cold temperatures, you are in no danger. When they <u>stop</u> hurting, you should warm and exercise feet until sensation returns.

Racks for hanging
clothes in your tent can be
improvised with saplings and rope, as
shown. Suspend saplings from ridgepole
near back of tent so that they
will be out of the way.

CAMPING TIPS 71

When extra hangers are
needed in camp for clothing, equipment,
etc., lash several forked sticks around
a tree. Similarly, forked sticks
secured to tent pole will hold gear
inside your shelter.

If you have no clothespins in camp to secure clothes to your line, use a piece of rope twice the length needed to reach between two trees or supports. Wrap the middle around one tree, then twist rope its entire length and tie the two ends to another tree. Laundry can be inserted between twists.

CAMPING TIPS 73

To keep first aid supplies dry and sterile on camping or fishing trips, place them in a plastic food bag, and seal end with a hot iron. The bag may then be stored in your pack or carried in your pocket.

Poison ivy leafs out
every summer to cause discomfort
to unwary campers and fishermen.
The common styptic pencil, dipped
in water and rubbed over inflamed areas,
will relieve the itching. Rub
on enough to leave a good
coating of the white
powder when it dries.

CAMPING TIPS 75

To treat skin affected by poison oak, ivy, or sumac, first wash area with a strong soap and then with alcohol. Apply a thick paste of melted soap to rash, let it dry, wrap area loosely, and let it remain overnight. Treat with calamine lotion thereafter.

A blister is likely to cause less trouble and heal more quickly if it is left unbroken. The skin and fluid over a blister is a safer and better bandage than any a camper can apply. If a fresh blister is broken, wash it with soap and water and cover with a sterile bandage.

CAMPING TIPS 77

Lockjaw can be transmitted through a cut or puncture made by a rusty nail, wire, fishhook, etc. So, as a precautionary measure, it's a good idea to get a booster tetanus shot before going on an extended camping, hunting, or fishing trip.

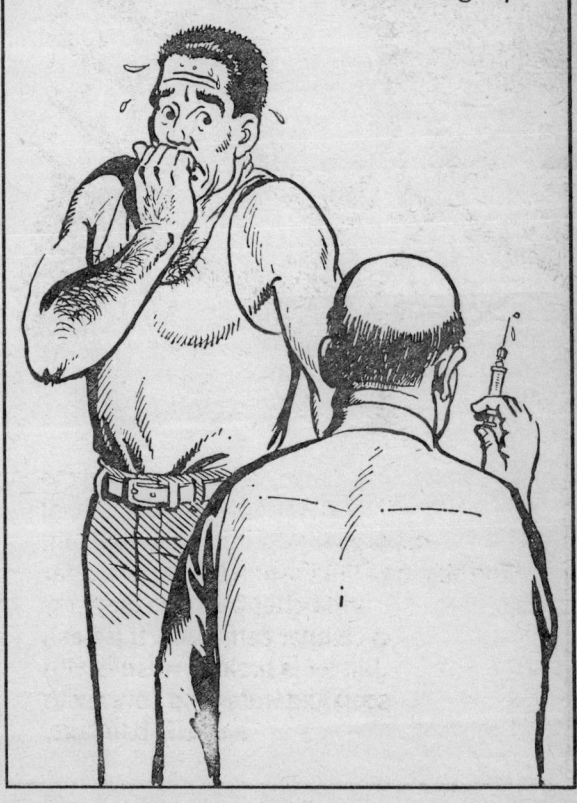

For packing into the wilderness
by foot, I try to keep the weight
of my complete outfit close to 40 pounds.
This is my minimum winter
clothing list: 1 lightweight
sleeping bag, 1 waterproof parka,
4 pairs heavy wool socks, 1 pair outer
mittens and liners, 1 cap with
earflaps, 1 pair light moccasins
for camp wear, 1 pair 8-inch
shoepacks, 2 pairs heavy underwear,
1 wool shirt, 1 cotton sweatshirt,
1 stocking cap for night wear.

CAMPING TIPS 79

The camper should never buy a sleeping bag covered top and bottom with plastic, rubber, or any other material that is completely waterproof. Body vapor will be trapped inside this airtight cover, and, no matter how warm or cold the weather gets, you will have a damp and clammy bed. The top cover must be porous enough to allow air to escape.

Several strips of aluminum foil under your sleeping bag will keep you warmer when bedding down on the ground. Newspapers will help if foil is not available.

CAMPING TIPS

Whenever possible, air and sun your camp bedding regularly. If it's a sleeping bag that zips only halfway and cannot be spread open, turn it inside out to sun it. This gets rid of moisture absorbed from the body or from rainy weather and makes the next night's sleep more comfortable.

To avoid having to dry-clean
your sleeping bag often, use an
inner lining of flannelette. This
extra blanket will add to the bag's warmth
and can be removed and cleaned
when necessary.

CAMPING TIPS 83

When camping overnight,
keep the clothes you plan to wear
the next day inside your sleeping bag.
They help fill the excess space and will
be warm the next morning
when it is time to dress.

It is best to clean a
down-filled sleeping bag by sponging
the dirty portions with lukewarm
soapsuds. Detergents and dry-cleaning
fluids tend to remove the natural
oils from the down and reduce
its resilience.

CAMPING TIPS

You may enjoy using an adirondack pack basket, which is light and well ventilated; however, it isn't moistureproof. Carry a light plastic covering in your pocket to throw over the pack when it rains.

Using the tumpline, experienced guides can carry heavy loads — over short portages — that would make a packhorse envious. But, before deciding on a tumpline to carry your gear, remember that it's a real chore every step of the way, and you'll need practice and conditioning before attempting it.

CAMPING TIPS

On back-packing trips an air pillow can be used as a headrest, a seat, or backrest. A small cloth bag with clothing stuffed loosely inside makes a comfortable cushion if you do not have an air pillow.

If your pack does not have straps
for carrying an ax, you can easily
sew them on one side. Reinforce inside of
loop to support weight of ax.
Loops are also handy for
hanging other equipment.

CAMPING TIPS

Hatchets, even when used by experienced woodsmen, can be dangerous, as they are light and easily deflected. A correctly hung ax head is slightly off right angle to handle.

YANKEE OR DAYTON

MICHIGAN

HUDSON BAY

NEW ENGLAND OR CONNECTICUT

A good camping ax should weigh about 2½ pounds, have a single bit, and a handle from 26 to 30 inches long. Get one with a sheath for the protection of both blade and camper.

Carrying an ax on your shoulder
can be dangerous. It is best to grip
it in one hand, near the head.
If you are on a slope, carry ax on your
downhill side; then, if you stumble, it can
be thrown out of the way.
Here is a simple double-bit ax
sheath made from leather and
pieces of inner tube.

CAMPING TIPS

A small section of rubber cut from an old inner tube can be used to cover your belt ax if you have no sheath. Cut tubing several inches longer than ax head, fold surplus over edges, and secure with a rubber band cut from tube.

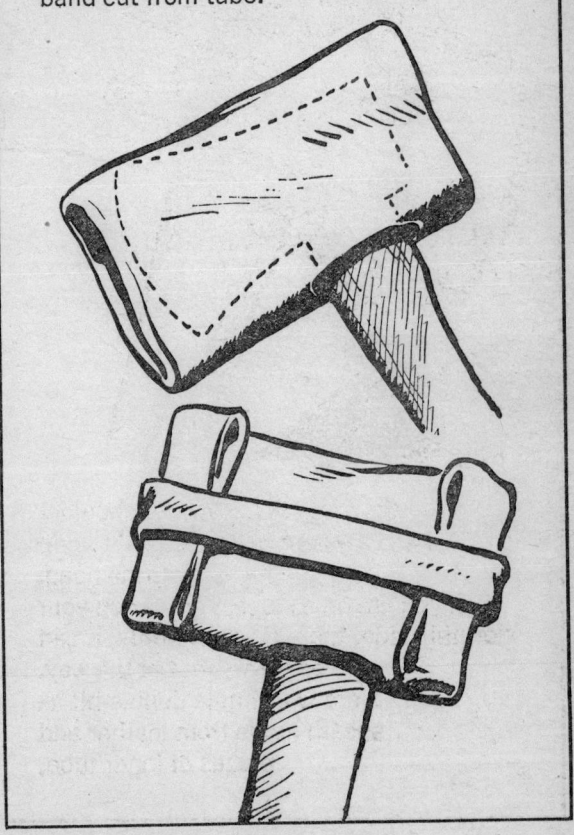

When sticking your ax in a stump or dead tree for safekeeping, always imbed it close to the ground. If it is high up, it can be knocked off in the dark and cause serious injury to camper.

WRONG

RIGHT

CAMPING TIPS 93

When packing your flashlight
for a camping trip, reverse the batteries.
Then, should the flashlight be
turned on accidentally, batteries
will remain fresh.

To keep your flashlight from accidentally switching on and burning out your batteries, place a round of cardboard between batteries and end of flashlight before storing it in your duffel. Reversing batteries may be only partial protection.

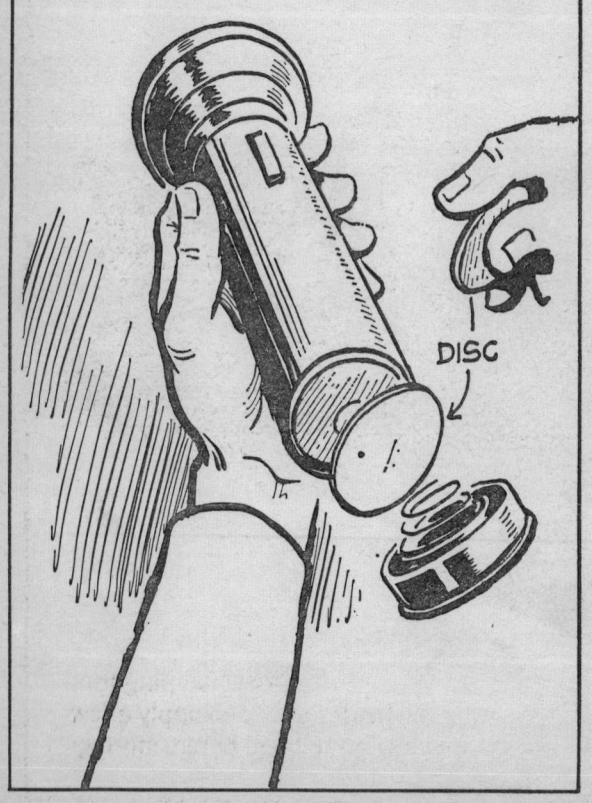

DISC

CAMPING TIPS

Knives should not be put away unless they are clean; acids and salts from your hands have a tendency to stain and mar blades.

After a camping trip, wipe the blades dry, then apply a few drops of oil to them before storing.

All knives carried in sheaths on the belt should be worn at the back. A fall could force the blade through leather and pierce the thigh if knife is worn in the front.

CAMPING TIPS 97

Binoculars may freeze at one setting during extremely cold weather, so adjust them to setting you expect to use and hang them under outer clothing. Also, camera shutters may work more slowly in cold weather, so use them at a faster setting than your light meter indicates.

When carrying your photography outfit on camping trips, remember that heat can be harmful to undeveloped film; avoid leaving film for any length of time in sunny places where heat may be concentrated.

An insulated bag, such as one used for keeping picnic foods cold, is a handy place for storing extra film.

CAMPING TIPS

For long-distance carrying of a crosscut saw, a length of garden hose split lengthwise and tied over the teeth of the saw will protect the edge and make it safe for handling. Burlap sacking may be wrapped around the saw if hose is not available.

Woodcutting at your permanent campsite can be more easily accomplished with a bow or pulpwood saw if you select the proper tooth pattern. The "four-cutter-teeth-and-a-raker" and the "bushman" patterns on a 30-inch frame will take a lot of work out of the job.

FOUR CUTTERS AND A RAKER

BUSHMAN

CAMPING TIPS 101

A half-inch elastic band fastened to your binocular or camera case, then wrapped around your waist, will prevent case from swinging loosely and getting in your way when climbing, gunning, fishing, etc.

To keep a valuable map from tearing at the creases, fold as desired, then unfold, cut along the creases, and paste on a sheet of muslin. Leave 1/8 inch between pieces for hinge action. A light coating of transparent varnish will protect map from moisture.

CAMPING TIPS

To relieve the discomfort of sore feet on the trail, lie down and elevate them when resting. Placing your tired feet on a heated rock wrapped in a shirt or towel will also bring relief.

Wear your pants legs on the outside of your boots when traveling in the woods. This will not only prevent moisture from seeping into boots, but will help to deflect the aim of a poisonous snake should you come upon one. Reflex action from dead snakes has caused accidents, so stay away from them.

CAMPING TIPS 105

Some vacationers who spend most of the year near sea level develop "mountain sickness" when ascending rapidly to high elevations. The symptoms are headache, nausea, dizziness, weakness, and sometimes diarrhea. Rest is all the treatment needed, but if symptoms persist, it's best to return to lower altitudes.

If you are caught in the snow
without proper equipment, try to
imitate the snowshoe rabbit:
Dig a hole in the snow deep enough for
your body to be protected from the
chilling wind; then crawl in
and let the drifting snow
fill in around you.

CAMPING TIPS

During extremely cold weather, should your hands and feet get cold in spite of thick mittens and socks, try adding insulation by stuffing shoes and mittens with cattail down stripped from dried stalks.

One of the safest spots
to be during an electrical storm
is inside your auto.
Do not stand on exposed hilltops,
near wire fences or other metal
structures, or under sparse trees. In the
woods you have the percentages
working for you — if
you keep away from the
tallest trees.

CAMPING TIPS 109

Here's a simple method for finding directions when lost. Push a stick (about 4 feet long) vertically into ground; using a small peg, mark the tip of the shadow cast by the stick. Wait 15 minutes, then mark tip of shadow with another peg.

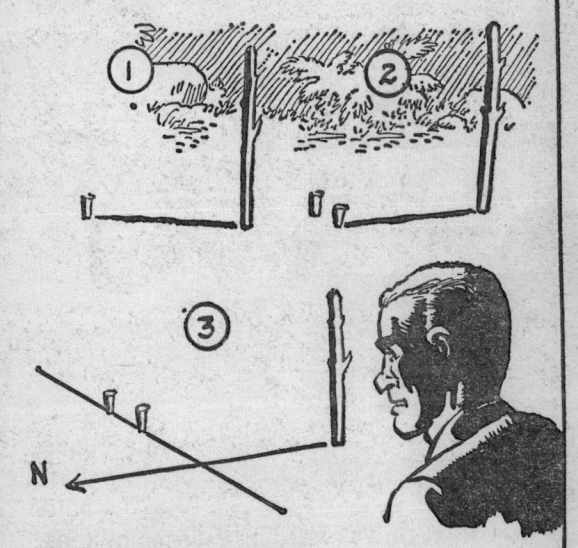

Draw a long straight line through the two marks as shown. Next, draw a line from base of stick extending at right angles across first line. The end of this line points to the north.

One method of finding directions should you be lost in the wilderness at night is to lie on your back under a tree and line up a branch on any star overhead (except the North Star). In a short time, the star will move directly west.

CAMPING TIPS 111

When traveling or camping in the wilderness, keep a safe distance from all wild creatures. Avoid loud noises and fast movements. If you come upon an animal unexpectedly, stand still a minute, then move slowly away. Never get an animal in a corner. Keep away from females with young.

If you are worried about bears entering your camp when you are away from it, try stretching a cord around camp area several feet above the ground. Then tie kerosene-soaked rags 4 or 5 feet apart along the line. The odor seems to be offensive to bears and may keep them away.

CAMPING TIPS 113

In areas where bears are located, be sure to wash out your canoe or boat after fishing, preferably with disinfectant, or the scent will attract bears, just as the salt in perspiration attracts porcupines.

Bears will rip canoes apart looking for fish, and porcupines will gnaw gunwales and paddles seeking salt.

Over most of North America the skunk is found in one of three forms: the striped, spotted, and hognose varieties. Should you be unfortunate enough to be tagged by one of these animals, you can remove the odor with a solution of 1 cup of household ammonia in a bucket of water.

CAMPING TIPS

Half-tame deer encountered in camping areas can be dangerous. Do not feed them, and do leave the young alone, for the razor-sharp hooves of the adults can inflict serious injury.

A good tip for car campers and boat enthusiasts who venture onto dirt roads with their trailers is to carry a foot-square section of 2-inch plank or a thin, solid metal plate. Then, if you have to change a tire in a sandy or muddy spot, you will have a solid footing for your jack.

CAMPING TIPS 117

Don't forget to carry
a set of wooden wheel chocks in
your trailer. Then, when you stop on
grades to take photographs or look at the
scenery, you won't have
to depend on roadside rocks to
anchor your vehicle.

Here are a few extras you should carry in your camping trailer for emergencies: a battery-type lantern with red flasher or blinker; several flares, in case of breakdown; weatherproof drop cords; a pair of wooden wheel chocks.

CAMPING TIPS 119

Trailer travelers should regularly inspect the lines and fittings of their propane–butane system, as vibration can cause leakage. While you are traveling, bottled gas should be turned off at the tank, as a leak inside the mobile home could be disastrous.

When trailer camping, have your rig equipped with twin propane tanks with a two-way valve for putting either of them into immediate service. With this setup, you'll know when you're running low and can have the empty tank filled at the first available place.

CAMPING TIPS 121

If you are trailer or station-wagon camping and are using a heater or stove that has a flame, be sure you have adequate ventilation. This is particularly true at high altitudes where oxygen is much thinner.

An extra ball for the
trailer hitch, attached to front
bumper of the towing vehicle, will make
maneuverability easier when you are
backing up in close areas. This is a
particularly good safety precaution
for autos towing boat trailers.

CAMPING TIPS 123

If your automobile door lock is frozen and you can't get the key in, try heating the key with a match or cigarette lighter.

USE PLIERS OR A GLOVE TO PREVENT HEAT FROM BURNING HAND

For added storage space when trailer camping, build your doorstep in box form to hold canned food, ammunition, tools, etc. For wiping shoes, cover top of box with rubber doormat material.

CAMPING TIPS 125

When beach camping remember these pointers:

1. Get permission from the proper authorities.
2. Check tide tables and study beach.
3. Take mosquito netting and bug bomb.
4. Be prepared for strong winds.
5. Support tent center pole and legs of cots with boards.
6. Use extra-long stakes.
7. Pile sand against tent wall to keep wind from blowing sand under floor.
8. Protect aluminum utensils, zippers, etc., from damaging salt air.

Mesh bags, from a purchase of oranges or onions, make good beach bags for children's toys. When you are ready to leave the beach or swimming area, just dunk the bag in the water to clean toys.

CAMPING TIPS 127

If you are planning to camp on a beach or on soft or sandy soil, carry along some tomato stakes to replace short tent stakes. If these don't hold, bury a log or stick at right angles to the pull, as shown.

128 MARK TRAIL'S CAMPING TIPS

Keep your eyes properly protected with some sort of hat or dark sunglasses when sunbathing. Your sensitivity to light when driving home at night can be reduced by more than a third after a day at the beach without sunglasses.